A Love Letter to Us

Poems on Black Love & Identity

By Ashley J.

Published independently by AJ Verse Publishing

A creative imprint dedicated to poetry, story, and soul.

Cover and interior design by the author

ISBN: 979-8-9941388-0-9

Printed in the United States of America

Foreword

Some voices shape us long before we understand why.

When I first memorized Langston Hughes in middle

school, something inside me shifted. His rhythm felt

familiar, like a truth I already carried. Later, Maya

Angelou taught me to rise with grace, and modern

poets showed me the power of speaking directly to

those who need it most. Those influences stayed with

me, as they do with many of us. Their honesty, their

courage, their tenderness- they echo through our

stories too. This book grew quietly over the years,

through poems written in still moments, thoughts I

held onto, and truths I learned slowly. These pieces

belong to every black girl who wondered if she were

enough, every black woman choosing herself, every

brother carrying more than he could ever say, and the

community that had always risen- softly, quietly,

together. *A Love Letter to Us* is just that: a letter

stitched with softness, strength, and becoming. I hope

that these verses help you feel seen. May they bring

you closer to the version of yourself you have been

quietly growing toward. One page at a time.

TABLE OF CONTENTS

To the Black Girl Who Needed to Be Seen

To the Black Woman Becoming

To Our Brothers, With Love

To Us, With Love

To the Black Girl Who Needed to Be

Seen

There is a girl inside every woman who once wondered

if her presence was ever meant to be noticed. These

words are for her- soft, steady, certain- a reminder that

she was never invisible, not even when the world tried

to dim her light.

Dear Black Girl

Dear Black Girl,

I wish you could see yourself the way the world was

never taught to-

how your presence softens a room

before you ever say a word.

Your curls, your curves, your brown eyes,

shaped by stories older than you.

Your sun-touched skin carries its own quiet glow.

None of it was ever an accident.

You were crafted with intention,

and molded with grace.

A marvel, long before you even knew your name.

Dear Black Girl,

You're not becoming worthy; you always were, even

when the world

 tried to tell you otherwise.

Dear Black Girl

You're more than beautiful.

You are a force,

a reflection of everything resilient and radiant-

a dream carried forward through generations.

Mirror Lessons

No one told her a mirror could lie,

but she learned anyway.

She learned that reflection and reality

are not always the same-

that sometimes the glass remembers

only what the world taught her to see.

She stood there searching for herself,

for the girl she was.

Before comparison became a habit,

and before her worth was measured

by someone else's comfort.

Before she knew the weight

of wanting to be enough.

The mirror caught her at her smallest-

in the moments where she forgot she came from

women who reshaped the world,

without asking for permission.

Women whose beauty was not up for debate, whose

faces carried history,

whose shadows held stories.

One day she'll learn

that the mirror isn't the authority,

It's just a surface, a moment,

a place she once mistook for truth.

Her real reflection?

It lives elsewherein her laughter, in her memory

in every room that lights up

just because she walked in.

May she one day see herself clearly

without the glass, without the apology.

And may she finally understand

that she was never the one who needed fixing.

It was the mirror-

it only reflected her image,

never her story.

Unseen

She was not invisible,

she was overlooked.

A girl standing in the open,

while the world's gaze slid past her,

as if she were made of glass.

She loved with a heart that kept reaching

for hands that never reached back,

learned to hold her hurt quietly,

and pretended the absence of care,

was not carving her into someone she did not

recognize.

But even in the loneliness,

some part of her refused to vanish,

a small, stubborn flame,

waiting for the moment someone finally realized, the

light they kept overlooking was hers all along.

The Weight of Too Much

The first weight she ever carried was a word that

didn't belong to her.

It was a single phrase handed to her

before she understood volume,

before she discovered that truth can be thunder to

those who fear the sound of it.

They told her she was too loud,

too bold, too bright.

Not knowing she came from a people

who survived by refusing to fold

into smaller versions of themselves

They wanted her quieter, contained-

not realizing some spirits were meant

to take up room.

She was never too much.

The world was just unprepared for a girl,

who carried that much power in her presence.

If Only Someone Told Her

If only someone told her,

that she didn't have to earn her place in this world.

That presence alone was enough,

that breath alone was proof of belonging.

If only someone told her

that worth is not a prize or a reward,

not something that was measured,

but something she carried

long before anyone noticed.

If only someone told her

that she didn't need to lose herself or

trade pieces of her spirit

to be accepted, to be understood.

If only someone told her

that rest was not selfish,

that dreaming was not luxury,

that her voice did not need permission to exist.

If only someone told her

she was always enough,

always worthy,

long before the world chose to see her.

Inheritance

She carried more than her name.

She carried a history that loved her first.

A lineage stitched into her being,

steady and unbroken,

woven through her spirit

long before she knew the word for legacy.

Her beauty was not a trend,

it was the return of everything that made her.

Her strength was not forced, it was inherited.

Her presence was not an accident,

it was the echo of women

who moved through storms

and still walked with their heads held high.

She was born with stories in her bones,

with glory humming beneath her skin,

with a truth too ancient to ever be erased.

She belonged to a people

who named her worthy

before she ever thought to question it.

The Tenderness She Was Owed

She met strength too early,

and gentleness too late.

The world handed her resilience

before it ever offered mercy,

taught her endurance

before it taught her rest.

She had to brace herself

when she should have been held.

To push through,

when she deserved to pause.

To silence her ache, when someone should have

spoken warmth into her name.

But tenderness,

had always been her birthright.

Not something to earn, not something to prove,

but something she should have known

from the beginning.

May she reclaim it now.

The ease, the warmth,

the freedom to simply be.

May she finally receive

the tenderness she was owed.

Girlhood, Reimagined

In another world,

her girlhood bloomed without interruption.

A season untouched by warning,

where joy arrived freely,

and lingered long enough to name itself home.

In that world,

no one taught her to brace for impact.

No one hurried her into the lessons

meant for later.

Her days unfolded softly,

not measured by survival, but by wonder.

She was allowed to exist

without translation,

without being asked to make herself less.

In that imagined childhood,

she moved through rooms,

without fear of being misunderstood,

without carrying burdens too heavy

for small shoulders,

without learning to decipher

the shift in someone else's mood,

before her own.

There, she was simply a girl.

Whole, loud, dreaming,

held by hands

that knew how to keep her safe.

May she return to that world

in the quiet moments,

and let the version of herself

who bloomed without interruption,

 remind her,

she deserved that all along.

To the Black Woman Becoming

Growth does not announce itself. It arrives in quiet ways- a softened posture, a steadier breath, the gentle decision to choose yourself once more.

For every woman who learns she is allowed to change, to rest, and to choose herself without apology.

The Black Woman

The foundation of mankind,

carrying so much courage,

so much wisdom.

Your beauty, your strength

surpassed by none.

The giver of life,

the one they doubted,

the one they labeled

before they listened.

But you became more

than anything they imagined,

more than anything they tried to limit you to.

You carried the parts of yourself

they never bothered to understand,

learned to trust your own reflection

when no one else offered truth.

You grew into your power with gentleness,

and no apology.

You are a Queen,

and you will always

reign supreme.

Heart of a Woman

The heart of a woman

is a place of knowing-

where identity deepens,

where a woman learns

the power of her own presence.

It's shaped by the journeys

that demanded patience,

the moments that asked her to ground herself,

and the wisdom that guided her

toward the woman she was becoming.

It holds the gentle teachings

shared from woman to woman,

the wisdom echoed through generations,

and the lineage of courage

resting in her hands.

And in that heart lives resilience-not loud, not forced,

but anchored, and her own.

For womanhood is not perfection,

nor the absence of fear-

It's the courage to step forward

with everything she is,

everything she'd gathered,

and everything she chooses.

Identity's Weight

In time, she came to realize

that identity carries its own weight-

not heavy, just constant.

Pieces of herself-

history, expectation, lineage -

shaping her quietly,

long before she knew their names.

She spent years learning how to carry it

not as a burden, but as part of her.

Something that rested

deep inside her,

and asked to be heard,

instead of feared.

There were parts of it

she couldn't grasp at first-

why certain wounds felt familiar,

why certain joys felt inherited,

and why some memories felt older

than her own experience.

Identity had a way of revealing itself slowly,

like a story unfolding

in the background of her life,

waiting for her to notice,

what it had been teaching all along.

With time, it became clear

that identity was not a weight

meant to hold her down-

but a compass, a quiet reminder

of where she came from,

and the woman she was free to be.

Rooted in Her Truth

She didn't grow into her truth

all at once-

it arrived slowly,

like a voice she'd forgotten,

calling her back

to the woman she was always meant to be.

It took time to unlearn the weight

of what others thought she should be,

to separate expectation from identity,

to trust the quiet pull

of what felt right in her spirit.

There were days she questioned herself,

days she stood uncertain,

days she softened her voice

just to keep the peace-

moments that taught her

what it meant

to live outside her truth.

But truth has a way

of rising through the cracks-

steady, unshaken,

refusing to be buried

beneath fear or doubt.

And when she finally listened,

she felt herself root deeply-not in who she was told to be,

but in who she had always been.

A woman grounded, clear,

and wholly her own-

rooted in a truth,

that could never

be taken away from her again.

Resilience Defined

She came to see

that some seasons arrive

without warning,

and she found

that something in her,

was already built to weather them.

It was the way she kept walking

even when the path felt borrowed.

The way she kept loving,

even if it felt scarce-

when she kept dreaming

in a world that tried to

name her small.

Her strength was not loud.

It did not roar,

it did not demand applause.

It lived in the soft places,

in the breath she steadied,

the boundaries she drew,

the truths she held

even when no eyes were there to see them.

Resilience for her,

was choosing herself again and again,

without asking the world

if she was allowed to.

Defined not by how she endured,

but by how she bloomed

in the very soil,

that tried to bury her.

Beneath The Skin

Beneath the skin,

there were things she never spoke of,

moments that settled into her memory

before she realized

that they would echo for years.

She carried the impressions left by people

who didn't handle her with care.

The unspoken expectations,

that made her question her instincts,

and fear that clung to her

long after she wanted to release them.

 And beneath that practiced calm,

the composure she rehearsed

long before it felt real-

lived a depth she protected.

A depth others mistook

because they never stayed long enough

to witness its strength.

She had been hurt

in ways she rarely admitted.

Healing was not graceful-

some days it pulled her under,

some days it gave her room to breathe,

teaching her slowly,

how to trust the ground beneath her.

Still, she reached for the parts of herself

that felt true,

even when doubt felt louder than confidence.

Still, she learned to own the pieces of herself she once

hesitated to claim.

Because beneath the skin

was not brokenness,

it was a woman piecing herself back together.

Born From the Deepest Roots

She was born from the deepest roots-

roots that remembered everything

even when she didn't .

Roots older than scripture,

older than memory,

older than the first name

her lineage carried.

Her ancestors whispered to the earth,

and it whispered back.

They prayed with their hands in the soil

because they knew

that God lived there, too.

Before she ever took her first breath,

they circled her,

marking her, blessing her,

placing in her chest a fire

that would not die,

no matter how many storms

tried to smother it.

She was born from women

who dreamed warnings,

saw signs in shadows,

and carried whole generations

in the quiet strengths of their backs.

Their tears became river water

in her veins.

Their prayers became the rhythm of her pulse.

Their unfinished stories

became the hunger in her bones.

She was the echo of every name

they were never allowed to speak,

The long-awaited answer

to a question whispered centuries ago,

the bloom in soil meant to bury them.

When she faltered,

their hands guided her.

When she doubted,

their wind filled her lungs.

When she broke,

they gathered the pieces-

not to remake who she was before,

but who she was destined to become.

For she was not just one woman.

She was a chorus, a constellation,

the living altar of everyone who loved her

long before she was born.

And when she finally stood,

whole, luminous, rooted and reaching,

the ancestors exhaled.

Because she was not simply born.

She was called forth.

Summoned.

Chosen.

Lessons That Stayed

In time, she came to see

that some lessons did not arrive as words-

they arrived as endings, absences.

As moments that pulled more from her,

than she knew she had to give.

And somehow, they stayed.

These lessons,

didn't make sense at first.

Not when she was young,

not when the world asked her to move faster than her

spirit ever could.

But years later, they returned to her as clarity,

arriving gently,

showing her the pieces she had carried

without understanding why.

Some of them hurt as they settled in,

but they rebuilt her anyway-teaching her what to release,

what to protect,

and the wisdom that was hers,

before she had the language to claim them.

In the end,

she came to know this;

not every lesson was gentle, and

not every lesson arrived with grace.

But each one shaped her-

whether it be refusal, fear, or silence.

What stayed became the foundation,

the voice she fought for,

grew into and finally claimed.

To Our Brothers, With Love

For the men who were taught to survive before they

were ever taught to feel- the ones who protected their

own hearts because the world was careless with them.

Here is space to breathe, to set burdens down. Here is

softness returned, and space to rest. You were always

worthy.

Brother, I See You

Brother, I see you.

I see the way you move through the world-

measured, aware, carrying more

than anyone ever admits.

I notice the pause before your words,

how you read a room

before letting even a fraction of yourself appear.

Not out of fear,

but because experience taught you

that being misread can cost

more than silence ever will.

I see the effort behind your calm,

the long exhale you never release,

the way you still show up

even when the day's emptied you.

Here, you don't have to brace yourself.

You don't have to pretend you're okay.

You don't have to shrink parts of you

that feel too heavy to explain.

Burdened Too Early

They placed responsibilities in your hands

before you even knew how much it would take from

you.

Told you to "be strong,"

to "step up,"

to "handle it,"

long before anyone asked

if you were ready or if you wanted to.

You learned to manage fear like a task,

to quiet your needs

so others could feel secure.

To grow faster,

than your heart could keep up with.

You moved through childhood

as if it was something

you had been hired to hold together-

rewarded for maturity

you never chose,

praised for resilience-

you grew because you had to,

not because you wanted to.

People saw your composure

and called it strength.

They never saw the cost.

They never noticed, how much you carried,

just to keep the world from falling apart.

Brother, none of what you endured

was your failure.

It was the weight of years

that asked too much, too soon.

And you survived it-

even when it asked you

to leave pieces of yourself behind.

I see all the versions of you-the guarded one,

the uncertain one,

the one growing,

the one grieving

the one simply trying again tomorrow.

And every version of you

is still worthy.

Every version of you,

deserves to be seen.

Childhood Interrupted

There is a version of you

that never got the years he deserved.

A boy should've had time to grow

gradually,

to learn himself before being asked

to understand everyone else.

But life didn't give you that option.

It handed you roles too big for your age, and you

stepped into them anyway-

not because you were ready,

but because someone had to.

You were expected to manage things

you were still trying to interpret.

Expected to bring calm

to situations that overwhelmed you.

Expected to be the rock,

before you ever felt solid.

People call you "mature,"

and praise how well you handled everything.

They missed the truth-

that handling wasn't the same as having help.

And growing up fast,

wasn't the same as being okay.

Pieces of your childhood slipped away slowly in all

the moments

 you learned to put yourself second,

because someone needed you first.

Brother, none of that was your fault.

Your boyhood did not fail-

it was interrupted.

And still, you continued forward.

Still, you became someone dependable,

someone thoughtful,

someone present.

That speaks to who you are-

not to what you were denied.

Armor

You move through the world

with a calm exterior,

a composed voice,

 a measured presence,

a look that tells people you are fine,

even when your mind is louder

than you let on.

And most people accept

that version of you.

They don't think to look past it.

They don't notice the hesitation

right before you answer a question,

or the way you pull back,

when conversations get too close.

You don't speak on what bothers you,

not because you don't feel it,

but because at some point you realized

that silence kept things from becoming bigger, than

they needed to be.

You've held yourself together quietly for so long,

that it almost feels natural.

But there's more to you

than what you show.

There's a man who feels deeply,

who thinks through everything before he says a word,

who wants connection,

but isn't always sure how to trust it,

or where to place himself inside of it.

You guard part of yourself carefully -

not to seem invulnerable, but to stay safe.

You're cautious with your emotions

because you've never been convinced

that they would be understood

if you showed them.

And still, I see glimpses,

small moments where the real you surface.

The softness you don't admit to,

the thoughtfulness you downplay,

the warmth that slips out

before you can pull it back.

You might not notice it,

but those moments say everything.

They tell the truth you rarely voice.

You feel more than you let on,

you want more connection than you ask for,

and you've learned to protect yourself

in ways most people never take the time to

understand.

I'm not here to dismantle the armor,

I'm not asking you to reveal anything.

I'm just acknowledging the man behind it-

the one who cares deeply

even in silence.

The one who figured out how to

shield himself,

long before he ever realized,

that he didn't have to do it alone.

Black Man, You are Allowed

Black man, you are allowed

allowed to feel what you feel

without turning it into something smaller.

You are allowed moments

where you don't have it all figured out.

Allowed to pause, to breathe.

Allowed to sit with what is happening inside you

without pushing yourself

to move past it too quickly.

You are allowed to want support

without seeing it as a flaw.

Allowed to lean when life gets heavy,

allowed to say what is weighing on you

without wondering if anyone

will take you seriously.

You are allowed to care

in the way you naturally do,

fully, honestly-

without burying it so no one notices.

 Allowed to hope for more

than routine and responsibility.

Allowed to want a connection

that meets you where you are.

You are allowed to be human-

not the version people expect,

not the role you stepped into for survival,

not the image you use to keep peace.

Human.

A man with layers,

with thoughts you don't always voice,

with needs you have learned to push aside,

with a heart that deserves to exist as it is,

even on the days you feel worn down.

Black man, you are allowed

to exist fully in your own life.

To want understanding, to want closeness,

to want a place where you don't have to carry

everything by yourself.

You are allowed all of this-

not because someone grants you permission,

but because it was always yours.

What You Come From

You come from people

who learned how to endure

without losing themselves completely.

From hands that built,

even when they were tired,

from voices shaped by time

before history had a name.

You come from patience,

from faith passed hand to hand,

from love that showed up,

even when it went unspoken.

From men who did the best they could

with what they were given.

From lessons learned the hard way.

From strength that wasn't loud,

but remained.

You carry that with you-

not as pressure, but as proof.

Proof that you are more

than what the world tries

to reduce you to.

More than a moment,

more than a struggle.

What you come from matters,

and who you are is enough.

For the Moments You Forget

This is for the moments you forget

how far you've come.

For the days when doubt speaks louder

than all you've carried.

When the world feels heavy,

and your efforts feel invisible.

Remember:

You didn't arrive here by accident.

Every step you took

required intention, courage, and restraint

most people never see.

You are not behind.

You are not less than.

You are not failing.

You've grown.

You've adapted.

You've kept going.

Even when stopping would've been easier.

So when the noise gets loud,

and your confidence wavers,

come back to this truth-

you are doing better than you think,

and you are exactly where you need to be.

For Your Heart, King

This was for your heart-

the part of you that kept choosing to be there

even when no one checks in on you.

Your heart has held patience.

It has held disappointment.

It has held hope longer

than anyone ever acknowledged.

It has chosen restraint,

when reacting would have been easier.

Chosen care,

when distance was expected,

chosen love,

even when it wasn't returned in full.

And still, it has not closed.

Still, it responds.

Still, it recognizes sincerity

when it is offered.

This was never about changing you,

or asking you to become anything else.

It was always about seeing you.

Every word before this was meant for you.

So this is for your heart, King-

not to harden it,

not to guard it further,

but to honor it.

And to remind you,

your heart,

exactly as it is,

has always mattered.

This was always for you.

To Us, With Love

For the aches we turned into lessons, the joy we carved

from the hard places, and the tenderness we are still

learning to trust. Here, our strength is honored, along

with the ways we choose one another through it all.

Together, we rise quietly, softly, and always as one.

Still Here

We're still here.

Not because it was easy.

Not because it was promised.

But because something in us stayed.

Through the nights that blurred together,

through mornings we didn't feel ready for.

We've learned to carry things

without making them our whole story.

How to lose parts of ourselves

and still recognize what's left.

There were moments we thought

this version of us wouldn't arrive.

Moments where surviving

felt louder than living.

And yet-

We're still here.

With softened edges,

with clearer boundaries,

with a deeper understanding of what matters,

and what can't get taken from us anymore.

We didn't come through untouched,

but we came through honest.

Still capable of joy.

Still capable of love.

Still here.

What Remains

What remains

is not the noise.

Not the urgency.

Not the versions of us

built for survival alone.

It's the pause before responding,

the instinct to listen first,

the quiet decision to not

take everything personally.

It's what didn't harden

when it had reason to,

what didn't disappear,

when it wasn't protected

What remains is a sense of self

that doesn't need to be proven.

The knowing that

we don't have to carry everything

just because we once did.

What remains,

is quieter than loss,

steadier than fear.

It's us-

without the excess.

Acknowledged

It happens in the pause between words,

in the way someone stays

without needing more from you.

Acknowledged-

not as performance,

not as a moment to be evaluated,

but as presence meeting presence.

Seen,

without being measured.

Met,

without expectation waiting behind it.

There is ease in that-

in not having to prepare yourself,

to be received.

Acknowledged for

what you carried without witness,

for what you held together

without anyone watching.

Nothing requested,

nothing extracted.

Just this-

someone noticing

and letting it be enough.

At Ease

There's a moment

when the body realizes

it doesn't have to be alert anymore.

The room stays still.

Time doesn't press forward.

Nothing arrives.

Nothing interrupts.

You're not bracing for anything,

and not holding space

for what hasn't happened yet.

At ease,

is existing without narration.

No lesson in it,

no meaning assigned.

Just you,

undisturbed.

Still Going

Still going.

No rush to it,

no pause either.

Just the act

of continuing.

Still going,

even when some days asked

for more endurance

than inspiration.

Still going,

without asking the moment

to explain itself.

Not because it's resolved,

but because stopping

never felt more honest.

Still going.

On Our Terms

We are no longer negotiating our peace,

our softness,

and our need for rest.

We've learned what it costs

to stretch ourselves thin.

On our terms

means we stop altering ourselves

for rooms that were never built for us.

It means we don't apologize,

for knowing what we need now.

We move

without asking permission.

We choose

without rehearsing justification.

This isn't defiance.

It's clarity.

It's deciding that what we protect

matters as much as what we pursue.

That how we live is as important

as what we achieve.

On our terms,

we keep what nourishes us,

we leave what demands too much,

and we trust what settled in us

over time.

This is the stance.

Quiet,

and unmoved.

And finally, ours.

With Intention

With intention,

we pause before agreeing,

before overextending,

before saying yes

to what takes more than it offers.

We notice

when our body tightens,

when hesitation appears

before language does.

That pause isn't restraint.

It's respect-

for our energy,

for our limits,

for the life taking shape without rush.

With intention,

we protect the unseen work,

the small decisions

that don't announce themselves,

but change everything.

This is how care looks

when it's practiced daily.

Not loudly,

not all at once.

Intentionally.

To Us, With Love

This was never about repair,

or asking ourselves to adjust,

or to change

so we could be accepted.

This was about seeing us clearly.

Without edits,

without conditions attached.

It was about honoring what we carried

without witness,

what we survived without applause,

and what we learned with no teacher.

This is for the parts of us

that stayed,

that softened without breaking,

that kept choosing ourselves,

even when it felt unfamiliar.

For the becoming,

for the unlearning,

for the moments we paused,

and decided differently.

To write this

not as an ending,

but as a reminder-

that we are allowed to arrive,

exactly as we are.

Nothing missing.

Nothing owed.

Just us.

Still here,

still becoming.

Sincerely,

To us, with love.

Author's Note

Poetry didn't arrive in my life all at once. It came

softly, the way truth often does-in childhood

memories that I didn't understand yet, in quiet

moments that stretched longer than they should

have, and in words that felt like breathing before

I knew why. For a long time, I didn't know where

the pieces belonged. I only knew they felt like

relief. Like peace. And somewhere along the way,

I realized these poems were never just a hobby.

They were a part of me, waiting to be claimed.

This collection comes from that place- from

softness I had to learn, from strength I didn't

know I was carrying, and from stories that lived

beneath the surface until they chose their

moment to rise.

Thank you for holding these words. And thank

you for letting them meet you gently, wherever

you are in your becoming.